747.0978 CAS
Castaneda, Eliza Cross.
Family home of the new West

DATE DUE

MAY 2 6 2009		
AUG 1 8 2011		
		ought.
GAYLORD		PRINTED IN U.S.A.

ELIZA cross castaneda

Family Home of
The New West

 NorthLand PubLishing

COVER: Photographs by Audrey Hall, Linda Hanselman, Heidi Long, Dave Rosenberg, and Pam Singleton.

FRONTISPIECE: A distinctive arched doorway opens into the softly lit hallway, where a pair of bright woven rugs leads the eye toward a colorful sunflower painting.

Text © 2006 by Eliza Cross Castaneda

www.northlandbooks.com

Composed in the United States of America
Printed in China

Edited by Claudine J. Randazzo
Designed by David Jenney and Larry Lindahl
Production supervised by Mike Frick

FIRST IMPRESSION 2006
ISBN 10: 0-87358-902-5
ISBN 13: 978-0-87358-902-4

10   09   08   07   06   5   4   3   2   1

Library of Congress Cataloging-in-Publication Data Pending

To my dad,
Gerald S. Cross,
who made sure
we never lacked for
good books,
good music,
and good art.

—E C C

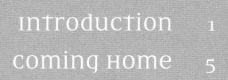

introduction

[OPPOSITE] It's a living space that would make Dr. Spock proud; long an advocate of the healthful benefits of fresh air and sunshine, the trusted pediatrician would appreciate how these homeowners found every opportunity to flood this dining area with natural light. Old-fashioned transom-style windows top the sidelight-flanked French doors, which can be opened to let in a breeze. The classic mission-style table and chairs are handsome, yet sturdy enough to withstand everyday use by a busy family.

In a tiny, packed-to-the-rafters mountain antique store, a tattered old board with peeling paint hung on a wall crowded with dusty portraits and faded mirrors. I had to squint to make out the phrase, painted on the sign long ago:

"Home is where your story begins."

Just six simple words, but they stirred me just the same. For whether you live in a city loft, a suburban tract house, or a remote cabin in the woods, home is where lives take shape, identities form, and memories are made. The very word "home" evokes strong associations and longings, which in turn shape and define our dreams for our own homes.

Creating a family home is no small order. Time becomes increasingly precious when children join the picture; priorities shift and design parameters usually follow suit. Functionality, organization, and "low maintenance" become key considerations, and practicality moves to the forefront of essential attributes as we strive to combine aesthetically pleasing furnishings that will also endure sticky fingers, spills, and the inevitable battery of toys.

The traditional nuclear family of the last century is an ideal as nostalgic as an Old West Calistoga wagon; these days, more than half of all families are "blended." As families have changed, so have our definitions of what a family home should be. Today's living spaces must often function for family members with widely varying ages, sometimes also accommodating the comings and goings of stepchildren and the diverse needs of extended families. At the same time, the home environment is constantly evolving as family members grow up. To cope with the ongoing challenge, we search for furnishings and materials that are flexible, adaptable, and beautiful—yet able to withstand the rigors of daily living.

Fortunately, homes in the "New West" tend to be less formal than their eastern counterparts, with a primary emphasis placed on comfort, warmth, and relaxation.

Home designs in this region commonly balance open, communal spaces with private areas where family members can relax and recharge. Westerners also tend to spend more time in the great outdoors, extending the living area outside for dining, entertaining, and recreation. Surrounded by fresh air, wide open spaces, and big skies, westerners increasingly make design decisions with an eye toward environmentally friendly applications and renewable materials.

You'll find inspiration from the homes in this book for everything from tiny details to major remodels. From the desert vistas of the Southwest to the high country panoramas of the Rocky Mountains, homeowners open their doors to share living spaces that are stylish and personal, yet inherently practical. You'll discover solutions to common challenges and ideas that translate to varying budgets, with the details and resources to help you develop your home's own personal style and character.

Welcome to today's family home of the New West. Step inside, and let your story begin.

[OPPOSITE] Massive timber beams and stone pillars create a natural backdrop for a rustic, softly curved chair topped with comfortable cushions, creating a soothing, shady oasis near the garden.

coming home

[*RIGHT*] Simple but highly functional, this indoor/outdoor transition area features weatherproof flooring, built-in log benches perfect for pulling off snowy boots, sturdy hooks to hang wet outerwear, and upper shelves for additional storage.

[*OPPOSITE*] Is there a warmer welcome than being greeted by the faces of those who missed you? These sturdy double doors feature heavy-duty hardware and handsome custom copper insets that help protect the lower frame from wear and tear; maximizing every opportunity to let the sunshine in, the upper frames are fitted with glass. Pretty potted flowers add a splash of color at the entrance.

Ah...the face of home. Who among us has not sighed with relief as we walked through the door, making the transition from the chaos of the outside world to the inner sanctuary of home? The front entrance establishes the family home's design style and creates a sense of cohesiveness between the exterior and interior. Because it makes such a strong initial impression, the entry deserves extra attention, from creating an appealing front walkway to keeping the porch clear of toys and sports equipment. Attractive landscaping, sturdy stairs, a comfortable place to sit, and good lighting all convey a sense of "welcome."

Traditional, rustic, refined or funky, no single element makes a more definitive design statement about the entrance of the western home than its front door. From the brightly painted doors of the Southwest to the time-worn reclaimed doors that grace many high-country homes, the front door is an important investment that must not only withstand the comings and goings of family members but also provide light and fresh air—all while barring the storms of winter and the heat of summer.

The old-fashioned parlor once served as the "receiving area" for the home, a role now relegated to the modern, high-traffic foyer. Warm lighting, a closet or peg rack to hang coats, a table to stow mail, and a thoughtfully placed mirror are all practical details that help create an inviting setting. Durable flooring is a must in the vestibule, and some active families opt for a separate "mud room" to keep snowy boots and outerwear confined to one area.

In homes where the front door is rarely used and family members go in and out through another entrance, the "everyday" entry area deserves as much attention and planning as the guest doorway. Even if it's the back door or a garage entrance, the area can be designed to be inviting and welcoming, a gracious gateway that reflects the unique face of your home.

[ABOVE] The pungent scent of juniper creates an aromatic welcome at this adobe home, where a cool courtyard beckons beyond a pair of wooden gates with unusual cut-work inserts. Potted geraniums and a pair of chile *ristras* add a punch of bright color. Good entrance lighting makes a home's entrance as hospitable at nighttime as during the day; when the sun goes down, the watchful eyes from these unusual metal sconces glow in the darkness.

[RIGHT] A simple entrance matches the serene setting of this Southwest home, where reclaimed doors and rustic sconces provide textural contrast to the smooth adobe walls. After inclement weather, muddy footprints can be easily hosed off the stone patio.

[RIGHT] A pair of rustic, reclaimed wooden doors is framed by an airy wrought iron arch and open sidelights in this doorway that gives visitors the sense of entering a secret garden. Flowers and fragrant herbs share garden space, making it convenient for the homeowners to make a quick trip to the garden to pick fresh herbs for dinner. The path is filled with crushed gravel, which also acts as a mulch to keep weeds at bay.

[BELOW] A sunny windowsill provides the perfect vantage point for the family cat to watch for loved ones to return home.

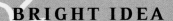

BRIGHT IDEA

[LEFT] Can a busy family ever have enough cubbies? This tricked-out mudroom features dozens of sturdy stacked cubbyholes that provide plenty of room for busy family members to stash everything during their comings and goings: shoes, boots, gloves, mittens, art projects, and homework. Soggy headwear can dry on the upper hat hooks and racks, while there is plenty of room on the floor to store footwear. The padded benches have concealed storage underneath, and a washable rag rug eliminates worries about muddy feet.

[RIGHT, ABOVE AND BELOW] Creating an immediate impression of the home's personality and family sensibilities, artwork, accessories, and framed photos are arranged—just out of the reach of curious little hands—on tables in each of these sunlight-filled foyers.

[OPPOSITE] This brightly painted front porch with its old-fashioned bench and inviting Adirondack chair seems to say, "Take off your shoes and sit a spell." Even a small front stoop can often accommodate a chair or bench, not only for seating but as a handy place to set packages while unlocking the door. A screen door lets cool breezes waft through the house and provides a glimpse into the vestibule, where a vintage mirror hangs over an antique chest topped by a small, glowing lamp and fresh flowers—extending the warm sense of hospitality inside.

[ABOVE] The inner door/outer screen door—and even the gutter—are painted a bright azure blue, creating a powerful impact at the front of this adobe home. Paint is an easy and inexpensive way to give a standard door design punch; notice how the decorative molding around the exterior of the door makes it appear larger.

[LEFT] In this vestibule, bright red is used to create dramatic impact on the wall just inside the door, where coat hooks, a simple metal bench, and stone tile create a stylish but practical outdoor-indoor transition area.

[OPPOSITE] Remember the color wheel from high school art class? Blue and yellow are classic complementary colors that make a vivid design statement in this light-filled foyer. Vertical columns and a row of small square windows contrast with the horizontal shadows and ceiling beams, and the corridor floor is the perfect spot for a collection of hardy, sun-loving houseplants.

[*ABOVE*] You'll never misplace your keys again if you have a table in the foyer to toss them on when you come home. An interesting collection of religious icons and candles of varying heights add visual interest, while tooled mirrors above the table reflect the light and are conveniently hung at eye level for a quick touch-up before leaving the house. A comfortable chair and a soft rug add to the welcoming mood of this space, and the sealed brick floors are an indestructible choice for families.

[*ABOVE*]   Even a plain entrance can be made more appealing with a few simple touches. Here, candles in glass holders—which prevent the flames from getting blown out—are arranged along the sill of a narrow window. A typical terra-cotta pot would have gotten lost against this adobe backdrop, but using a generously-proportioned container with a bright blue glaze adds a knockout punch of contrast and color.

[*RIGHT*]   Colorful hand-painted tiles add an unexpected accent on these stairs, and have the added benefit of eliminating shoe marks on the risers. The wrought iron handrail is a handsome accent that was designed for safety, with minimal distance between the spindles. The durable glazed Saltillo tile floor perfectly fits the mood of the house and is an excellent choice for a busy foyer; a large, wrought iron chandelier provides abundant illumination for the entire area.

[ABOVE] The morning sun streams through this inviting home's entrance, enhanced with large freestanding pots of plants, hanging flower baskets, and an appealing arrangement of outdoor furniture.

[LEFT] This wicker chair with its plump striped cushions is not only confortable, it's also a practical dropping-off place for bags and packages when opening the front door.

[OPPOSITE] The lines between outside and in are blurred in this vestibule, with its natural timber columns and twig stair railings. The antique chest has plenty of drawers to neatly hold the family collection of hats, gloves, and mittens that so often get jumbled in a coat closet.

Cooking & Gathering

The "heart" of the home, the kitchen—more than any other room in the house—draws people together. A natural gathering place and the hub of a busy family, a well-designed kitchen engages all the senses, from the warmth and good aromas wafting from the oven to the happy sounds of laughter, clanking pans, and conversation; to the flavors of nourishing, home-cooked meals, and an overall sense of well-being and comfort.

Today's kitchens are often outfitted with professional appliances and accoutrements for serious chefs, and these elements must be balanced with functionality and safety. Because of the kitchen's myriad roles, an efficient layout and adequate storage are important elements to creating a practical and enjoyable space. The inherent hazards for small children must be considered in the family kitchen as well. One solution is to incorporate an island or peninsula that not only serves as a practical area for storage and food preparation, but also creates a natural barrier that allows children to be present, yet protected from hot cooking surfaces and sharp knives.

Western kitchens are often designed with abundant windows, an arrangement that presents a unique challenge in locating cabinetry, but provides the benefit of flooding the space with natural light. Additional task and ambient lighting will enable the room to be highly functional for a variety of uses, and durable countertop materials and flooring that can withstand daily traffic will allow all family members to enjoy the kitchen without the worry of spills and stains.

It's a well-documented phenomenon that everyone gathers in the kitchen during a party, and accordingly, the room plays an additional role as an entertaining center. In-kitchen seating, a variety of work areas, and a floor plan that allows for good traffic flow will enable guests and family members to interact and enjoy each other's company while still allowing plenty of space for food preparation.

[ABOVE] Shish kebabs straight from the grill are ready to be served as an easy, informal family dinner.

[OPPOSITE] Expansive windows face the backyard in this sunny, light-filled kitchen, allowing parents to keep an eye on the children outside during meal preparation. A large butcher block table serves multiple functions; when it's not being used for food preparation, it provides a sturdy surface for homework and school projects, plus seating for up to eight people.

[*ABOVE*] "The art is in the details" in this distinctive kitchen, where a pitched pinnacle over the kitchen cabinets houses accent lighting and mirrors the shape of the bookcase in the adjoining room. The knotty pine cabinetry is trimmed with strips of contrasting wood and natural bark.

[*RIGHT, TOP*] The cabinets are located along the walls of this oversized kitchen, leaving plenty of space in the middle for a family dining table and work island. A hanging pot rack keeps pans handy at arm's reach, and the walls are decorated with a colorful collection of plates.

[*RIGHT, BOTTOM*] Instead of a matched look, the cabinets are painted in two complementary colors—a warm cream and a soft sage green. No soffits here, either; the homeowners opted to use the space above the cabinets for additional storage. A farm-style, fire-glazed ceramic kitchen sink is deep enough to wash the dog, and the gooseneck faucet is handy for filling large containers like stockpots and watering cans.

[*OPPOSITE*] The kitchen opens right onto the patio and yard, making it easy to call the kids for dinner. The butcher block top is a durable and practical choice for the island; most butcher block surfaces require just a monthly wipe-down with mineral oil to maintain the wood, and any small nicks and stains can usually be sanded out. A standing plant basket takes up just a couple of feet of floor space, but holds a sizeable collection of cookbooks.

[*RIGHT*] The home fires burn bright in this cozy kitchen, where a corner fireplace provides warmth and can even be used to toast marshmallows. S'mores, anyone? An island with a heavy butcher block top provides a large work area, and a separate sink makes food preparation a breeze.

[*FAR RIGHT*] A professional-style stainless steel stove has plenty of burners, a griddle, and double ovens to handle the multiple demands of cooking for a large family. A countertop LCD television allows the cook to watch the news—or a favorite cooking show—right in the kitchen. The unique corner windows look out on the adjacent patio, which includes a separate outdoor fireplace.

BRIGHT IDEA

[*OPPOSITE*] A round table is the friendliest arrangement for family conversations, where everyone can see each other; these curved chairs are designed to fit nicely around the table. The circular theme is continued through the spherical designs on the rug and the round light fixture above the table. The white cabinetry is especially durable and can be easily wiped clean. A collection of colorful ceramics can be seen through the glass-fronted cabinets; a combination of open and closed shelving provides plenty of storage, including clever built-in wine racks.

[*RIGHT*] Good lighting is a key component of a functional family kitchen. In this room, natural sunlight is augmented by colorful pendant lights, and additional ambient light is supplied by recessed lighting and a ceiling mounted track light. The glossy black granite countertops are handsome and functional, and have the added benefit of being virtually indestructible.

[ABOVE] This space is warmed by not one, but two fireplaces—both raised off the floor for increased safety and efficiency. Vivid blue tile—impervious to spills—covers the countertops, and the floors are equally tough Mexican tile.

[OPPOSITE] Art and functionality peacefully coexist in this colorful kitchen, where halogen lights illuminate the art, and also provide adjunct lighting for cooking. The subway-style tile backsplash is easy to wipe down, and the wall-mounted utensil rack makes good use of space. (Note the white, wall-mounted cubes, perfect for displaying small art pieces.)

[ABOVE] Simple and functional, this kitchen features a butcher block counter rounded to avoid sharp corners for small heads. Open cabinets not only provide display space, but they also make it easy to get to the dishes. A hanging rack is tucked under the cabinet near the stove, and the area above the cabinets is used for storing large items such as stockpots. A restaurant-style hose sprayer makes fast work of a sink full of dishes.

[LEFT] An unconventional way to bring color into a room, these whimsical chairs are hand-carved and painted with bright Mexican folk art designs. Colorful tile accents surround the island/countertop and backsplash. A spacious pantry cabinet offers plenty of storage, conveniently located next to the refrigerator.

[LEFT] This kitchen proves that a sleek, contemporary design can co-exist with family-friendly elements. Notice how much the apple green color impacts this space; modern, hard-working design elements include the sturdy wire mesh bar stools, pendant lights, and tough-as-nails granite countertops. Extending the counter along the wall creates a ledge for display space, up high and away from small hands.

[RIGHT] These slab cabinets of handsome, natural-finished maple speed up kitchen cleaning since there are no moldings to attract dirt and grime. A huge pantry area adjacent to the main kitchen has enough cabinet space to store rations for a small army.

[LEFT] The retro diner-style swivel stools give this kitchen a sense of fun, and in case the swiveling gets out of hand, the wainscoting on the toe-kick area is reinforced with a contrasting band of industrial "quilted" stainless steel. To duplicate the finish, which is also repeated in the backsplash, look in the telephone directory for "steel fabricators" or "restaurant supply." Track lights are tucked unobtrusively into the ceiling rafters, supplemented by a pair of industrial-style pendant lights.

[BELOW] A space-saving breakfast bar of polished granite is designed so the stools can slide underneath. A niche built into the back riser creates a space for condiments or a perfect bowl of fruit. A cozy nook just through the archway allows for guests to congregate comfortably, but still be near the action of the kitchen.

[RIGHT] Woodsy and warm, standing-dead Douglas-fir timber columns define this rustic kitchen, and handcrafted twig barstools surround a hefty slab wood countertop. Amber glass pendant light fixtures give the room a warm glow, augmented by recessed and undercabinet lighting.

[OPPOSITE] In this open kitchen space, the family opted to create one lo-o-o-ong island that not only provides abundant work space, it also serves as a sideboard for the adjacent dining table. The oversize, vintage farm-style porcelain sink is large enough to bear a meal's worth of dishes.

[*LEFT*] An unusual round peninsula, just the right size for a platter of party food, juts out from one end of this breakfast bar. A trio of pendant lights illuminates the countertop, and slate floors in mottled tones are a great choice for the kitchen floor—perfect for hiding spills and crumbs.

[*OPPOSITE*] A colorful, open kitchen was designed to serve many functions for this busy family including plenty of counter, table, and seating space; a desk area for homework and bill-paying; and a bench for relaxing. Some of the cabinetry has a natural finish, and the rest was painted in shades of cream and sage green. The island cooktop was designed with a recommended safety feature, a "landing" space on either side for hot pots and pans.

[*ABOVE*] This curved kitchen counter is not only distinctive, it allows for more seating; the wrought iron stools are covered with durable kilim rug fabric. A swagged antler chandelier and a stained glass window inset give the room a historic Old West feeling, and the modern stove hood, covered in wood, almost looks like an antique.

29

BRIGHT IDEA

[*LEFT, RIGHT*] A dedicated baking station provides a convenient place to store a stand mixer
plus all of the necessary measuring cups, bowls,
and baking dishes. The arched window provides a
dramatic accent over two standard windows, and
allows natural daylight to flood the baking area.

[*LEFT*] "Curves ahead" in this stylish
kitchen, where a rounded peninsula
creates additional work space and a
handy shelf for cookbooks is tucked
at the end. Natural cherry cabinetry
is accented with simple iron hardware;
glass-fronted cabinets with built-in
lighting illuminate pretty glassware.

[ABOVE, LEFT] A small light was wired to the side of a cabinet so that the cook can make full use of the work space and enjoy the glorious view.

[ABOVE, MIDDLE] A mullioned window is used as an artistic, one-of-a-kind space divider, and each hand-painted masterpiece lets the light shine through.

[ABOVE, RIGHT] Pickled wood contrasts with knotty pine in these simple, rustic cabinets, topped with a thick butcher block countertop. Glass-fronted cabinets show off the owner's collection of ceramic dishes and glassware.

[LEFT] A hard-working chandelier doubles as a pot rack to hold a handsome set of shiny copper cookware. Under-cabinet lighting illuminates work spaces on the counters, and also creates a dramatic effect at night.

[*OPPOSITE*] A stainless steel hood is handsome, but it does require regular cleaning to remove fingerprints from its shiny surface; instead, this family opted to camouflage theirs with rock masonry. Dual sinks allow more than one cook to work on a meal, speeding up meal preparation.

[*LEFT*] Rustic and elegant styles contrast beautifully in this open kitchen, with its hand-hewn timbers and refined cabinetry. The dining table's styling is formal enough for dinner parties, but its easy-care, lightly distressed surface means it's casual enough to eat on every day. The shades on the overhead chandelier can be removed for a more elegant look.

[LEFT] Appliances that look like antiques—but with modern controls and power elements—were chosen for this simple kitchen, with its straightforward collection of dishes and pans stored on a primitive open wood shelf. An unusual wood and glass chandelier hangs overhead, complementing the handcrafted twig railing that borders the room from the loft above.

[BELOW] A weighty pair of bookends can create a space for cookbooks anywhere; here, charming moose bookends complement the bronze patina of the sink hardware.

[OPPOSITE] Leaving the brick exposed was an excellent choice in this urban kitchen; the walls don't need maintenance, the surface hides fingerprints—and it looks great. Tall cabinets were chosen to maximize storage space; note the row of undercabinet drawers perfect for storing the small miscellaneous items that so often end up in the "junk drawer."

[ABOVE] The simplicity of this room's pale cabinetry and soft plastered walls creates a pristine backdrop for fancy details like the ornate carved cabinetry accents and hood surround; randomly placed mosaic tile covers the backsplash.

[OPPOSITE] When a mountain home has gorgeous kitchen views, it's worth sacrificing some of the overhead cabinetry for windows. This oversize island covered in weathered barnwood provides ample storage, a large counter space for food preparation, and even seating space to slide in a set of unique saddle-shaped stools. A wrought iron rack for pots and pans hangs overhead.

Dining Together

The family dining table has a way of uniting even the busiest of families. With our tightly-scheduled and activity-packed lives, sharing a meal together at the table is a ritual that is more important than ever. The family table is often where a lot more than eating takes place: homework gets done here, the newspaper is spread out and read, art projects and masterpieces are created, pie crusts and cookies are rolled out, and offhand talking leads to meaningful discussions.

A casual table in the kitchen allows for quick breakfasts, weekday dinners, and snacks. A breakfast bar, seating along one side of an island, or barstools along a raised kitchen counter are also practical options for informal eating. A built-in banquette or booth can be another space-saving way to squeeze in kitchen seating. When children are small, a spot to pull up high chairs and seating that accommodates booster seats plus easy-to-maintain surfaces and washable table coverings will make mealtime less stressful and more enjoyable for everyone.

While some homes have a little-used "formal" dining room reserved for large groups or holiday entertaining, many western families are opting to create a casual, separate space for everyday dining. A round table is best for encouraging conversation and allowing everyone to see each other, but it limits the number of guests that can be comfortably accommodated. A rectangular table, on the other hand, offers more versatility for large groups, especially if the table can expand or shrink with the addition or removal of adjustable leaves. Lighting is an especially important consideration in the dining room, and a combination of central, over-the-table lighting, plus dimmable lights can best accommodate different occasions and changing moods.

Sometimes adjunct dining spaces can be tucked away in unexpected places—a quiet nook or alcove, for instance—to allow for spontaneous or intimate dining when the whole family isn't present. A table for two is a perfect spot to share a morning cup of coffee or enjoy a candlelight dinner.

[ABOVE]   A path of river rocks flows through this kitchen dining area, creating a break between the tile kitchen floor and the hardwood dining floor. Bright turquoise blue paint gives new life to an old table and creates a striking centerpiece for the room.

[RIGHT]   To achieve the pebbly, bottom-of-the-river look, the homeowners painstakingly placed each stone by hand.

[BELOW] Spare and natural, benches and chairs maximize seating space around the table in this log home's cozy dining nook, which was designed to protrude from the house to create a sense of being both inside and out. The simple accents include cheery green plaid seat cushions and an overhead light accented with pine branches.

[ABOVE] A modern take on the classic picnic bench, this elegant stone table is trimmed in airy iron scrollwork. Nearby, a comfortable banquette with pillows provides additional seating and storage space underneath.

[ABOVE & RIGHT] Antiques and contemporary pieces combine beautifully in this in-kitchen dining area. The old, beat-up chairs—some are even missing spindles—get a unified look with a coat of bright blue paint. The simple pine table top complements the natural, unstained knotty pine window trim. Whitewashed wainscoting runs horizontally on the walls, and the working wood burning stove is energy-efficient for cooking and heating. An old-fashioned transom window above the door can be opened for ventilation.

[OPPOSITE] The curves of the contemporary, upholstered yellow dining chairs accent the round table in this bright and sunny dining area, situated by a large bank of windows. The ceilings soar, but the bold painting on the adjacent wall and the dark circular rug anchor the space and help make it feel more intimate. (Notice the unusual filler at the bottom of the floral arrangement's vase? Not only do the lemons provide a bright color accent, they help hide the stems of the flowers.)

BRIGHT IDEA

[*OPPOSITE*]   This homeowner devised a clever solution to the problem of the family dog begging for scraps during mealtime; a pet bed is thoughtfully built into the floor-to-ceiling wall of custom cabinetry. Although the room has abundant woodwork, the handsome stone floors help to lighten the space and keep it from feeling too dark; fitting both the fronts and backs of the cabinets with glass also brings in more sunlight.

[*ABOVE*]   Cowhide is a material commonly used in western design, but it's also one of the toughest and sturdiest forms of natural leather—making it an ideal upholstery choice for families. Here it's used to cover four rustic chairs that are pulled up around a casual painted wooden table. The black and white tile floor is easy to clean and it also camouflages crumbs and spills.

[*LEFT*]   For worry-free family dining, it's tough to beat a rustic design scheme. In this room, hand-peeled log chairs with seats of cowhide provide an eclectic contrast to the traditional rug, which protects the hardwood floors from scuffing as the chairs are pulled in and out.

[*ABOVE, LEFT*] Painting one wall of this dining space deep burgundy adds richness and drama to this dining space; leather chairs are elegant, but tough, long lasting—and imminently practical.

[*ABOVE, RIGHT*] Sometimes a dark wood table and chairs can dominate a modest dining space, but this room is a perfect example of how painting the walls a light color—in this case, soft butter yellow—can keep the furniture from overwhelming the room.

[*LEFT*] Seating for twelve? Windsor-style chairs surround a generously-proportioned country pine table, and when unexpected guests drop by, a quartet of barstools at the counter can be put into service.

[*OPPOSITE*] Evoking memories of Grandma's house for Sunday dinner, the contemporary design of this airy room contrasts with the antique dining table and chairs and lace tablecloth. The china hutch is positioned in the corner, away from foot traffic.

[LEFT] These chairs feature seats of tightly hand-woven fiber rush, a covering which has endured for centuries because the material is strong, durable, and comfortable. Two serving tables near the dining table can hold trays of food during large family meals, freeing the eating surface from clutter.

[LEFT] Mealtime can't help but be peaceful in this room, with its commanding views of the mountains, lake, and patio. The dining chairs are covered in black leather and trimmed with unusual fringed accents, and a piece of glass was cut to fit over the round table to protect its leather-topped surface from spills.

[RIGHT] When the French doors are thrown open in this family dining room, fresh scents and sounds of breezes rustling through the pine trees fill the air. A collection of antique chairs surrounds a sturdy, timeworn table, with comfortable, curvy armchairs at the head and foot of the table for the host and hostess.

[OPPOSITE] Dark floors, furnishings, and woodwork contrast beautifully with the pale walls and large windows in this high country home. Comfortable chairs surround a simple round table, and a massive overhead chandelier is accented with pine branch detailing. The nearby window seat with plenty of pillows provides additional seating and a relaxing spot to enjoy the beautiful views or for children to play while the adults savor long conversation at the table.

[ABOVE] The focal point of this dining room is a kalim, a long wooden antique table, surrounded by a collection of sturdy chairs. The homeowner commissioned a custom, removable tin top to fit over the table. A wrought iron chandelier and a cozy fireplace provide warmth and light at night, and the angel hanging over the fireplace was a flea market find.

[LEFT] Enduring mission-style furnishings feel right at home in this classic bungalow dining area. Lace café curtains covering the bottom half of the windows afford privacy while still allowing the light to shine through the upper windows. Notice how the chandelier picks up the shape of the lampshade on the sideboard.

[OPPOSITE] An upper-story dining room overlooks the treetops, and the round table is topped with an unusual chandelier with lights that look like a ring of wax pillar candles. The rock fireplace burns brightly on chilly winter evenings, and the peaked angle of the fireplace niche is repeated in the adjacent window.

[ABOVE] A trio of comfortable leather-upholstered log chairs surrounds a rustic table in this intimate setting. Its proximity to the windows lets parents or grandparents enjoy a relaxing meal and still keep an eye on the children outside.

[RIGHT] Secluded and cool, a small table and stools just fit in this home's wine cellar, providing a serene setting for private wine tastings and quiet dinners.

Living & ReLaxing

We ask a lot of the family living room: we want it to be stylish, yet relaxed; calm and quiet for reading and conversation, yet equally able to handle noise and roughhousing when children are about; handsome and good-looking, yet easy-going enough that we can put our feet up at the end of a long day. Fortunately, it's possible for all of these attributes to coexist in a well-planned living area.

While the traditional arrangement of a formal living room paired with an informal family area is still quite common, increasingly, homes in the West have a central, open living space or "great room." With either floor plan, the best living spaces invite family interaction and relaxation, and provide plenty of comfortable seating for family members to engage in a variety of activities.

The living area tends to be a place of transition, so it needs to be versatile enough to change according to the varying needs and interests of family members. When children are small, life will be easier if the room is child-proofed with breakables packed away or put out of reach. Unfussy furnishings upholstered with tough, washable fabrics or removable covers are best suited for family living areas that get a lot of use; if pets are on the furniture, patterned or textured fabrics can help hide daily wear and tear. Older children may be encouraged to spend more time at home if the room is designed as a comfortable area for watching television or listening to music; some families have dedicated media rooms for this purpose.

A fireplace is often a major design element in the western living room, which creates a natural focal point that calls for comfortable—but safe—seating around the hearth. Large windows that bring in abundant views and let the sunshine in are an asset that will also dictate choices in window coverings and lighting that adjust to different times of day and varying activities.

[LEFT] A large armoire hides the television, stereo, and clutter, and even features a lighted, protected area to display a valuable piece of art.

[RIGHT] A beloved family photo can easily be transferred to cloth and stitched onto a pillow; just look for photo transfer sheets for fabric at an office supply store. After scanning and printing the photo on the paper, simply iron the image on the fabric.

[BELOW] An antique wooden trunk makes an excellent coffee table. Any scuffs and nicks will only add to the charm of its time-worn surface, and it also provides additional storage for the living area. A pair of comfortable chairs is covered in America's favorite blue jean fabric—sturdy denim.

[OPPOSITE] When a fireplace hearth is at floor level, a fold-out screen provides protection from heat and sparks. Built-in bookshelves surrounding the mantle provide plenty of storage and display space. The furnishings, artwork, and area rug all reflect the same color palette of muted earth tones, and the varying patterns and textures of the furnishings better hide the inevitable stains and spills.

[LEFT] Indian rugs create a striking design scheme in this comfortable room, where rich reds and browns are set against a backdrop of neutrals. The red plaid curtains can be pulled to block the light from the patio doors, and a pair of wicker chairs and an ottoman create a separate conversation or reading area.

[OPPOSITE] They say variety is the spice of life, and this room combines a mixture of eclectic elements that blend into a beautiful living area. A quirky marionette hangs in the corner, overlooking a child's tea set and a pair of sofas slipcovered in vintage-style fabric. The Indian rug, antique furnishings, and whitewashed brick walls add to the sense of the room's storied past.

[RIGHT] Why shouldn't the men of the house have their own space to relax? Here, a pair of oversize leather chairs shares an ottoman—and a splendid view of the outdoors; the thick window ledge displays a collection of hats. Carved nightstands are just the right height to use as side tables, and they include storage underneath, too.

BRIGHT IDEA

[ABOVE]   Create separate living areas within the same room. In this family living space, one grouping is created with two oversize easy chairs and an ottoman for a comfortable conversation area around the hearth. Another area is created with a couch, two chairs, and a glass-topped coffee table. The bookshelves hold a large collection of books, photos, and art pieces, and the library ladder makes it easy to reach the tallest shelves.

[RIGHT] This cube storage unit was mounted horizontally to the wall, creating display space within and a surface on top for an arrangement of framed pictures, objects d'art, and a small lamp. The frosted glass doors are hand-painted to coordinate with the room. Tall, vertical flower arrangements help create visual balance.

[ABOVE LEFT] This room proves that "formal" doesn't have to be fussy. Two slipcovered couches are arranged at right angles, and a pair of traditional armchairs rounds out the seating arrangement. The vertical columns of framed black and white photos add a contemporary contrast to the antique mantle and marble fireplace surround.

[ABOVE RIGHT] When it's not being used for "Hide & Seek," an armoire with a large upper shelf is a perfect spot to hide the television or stereo equipment.

[ABOVE] Fun and funky, this "rec" room reveals much about the family's interests with surprising elements like the framed gold records and globe collection, plus retro furnishings including the narrow surfboard-style table, leather butterfly chairs, and lava lamp.

[LEFT] This small space seems much larger due to the distinctive half-moon leaded glass window installed in the peak of the ceiling. An antique dresser just fits in the space next to the fireplace, and the French doors can be opened to expand the living area out onto to the awning-covered deck.

[OPPOSITE] The simplicity of this room gives it a peaceful feeling, and an expanse of windows captures the views of the surrounding countryside. A bench topped with two cushions provides seating and side table space in one piece, and a flotaki rug underfoot provides soft textural contrast. The doors open out onto the porch so family members can be indoors and outdoors, yet still have a sense of togetherness.

[RIGHT] Red is a natural accent color against dark wood, and this room embraces the winning combination with a lipstick red leather couch and crimson patterned curtains. Visitors are welcome to put their feet up on the old, rustic coffee table and take in the great views, and a moose lamp provides accent lighting—but you might also see the real thing strolling by the window.

[LEFT] No engineered rocks for this hearth; the mason built the massive fireplace the old-fashioned way, with smooth granite river rocks placed by hand. An antique chest under the coffee table provides storage to keep the tabletop clutter-free, and an old quilt protects the leather couch from sticky hands and enthusiastic dogs.

[LEFT] No matter how cold it gets outside, this living room is always cozy with its river rock hearth and plenty of windows for weather-watching. A comfortable rocking chair, leather furniture, afghan blankets for curling up, and hardwood floors topped by an old-fashioned rag rug add to the room's sense of warmth.

BRIGHT IDEA

[ABOVE] This family designed a pass-through log box right next to their fireplace. There is a door outside next to the woodpile where the logs get loaded. No more mess!

[*OPPOSITE*] A living area in the master suite gives the parents a private space to relax, and the couch was arranged at an angle to capitalize on the warmth from the fireplace. A desk in the corner provides a quiet place to practice the lost art of letter-writing, and when the homeowners want to sleep in they can draw the curtains to block the sunlight.

[*ABOVE*] This loft's multipurpose room can handle a lot of living; the open area includes a pair of comfortable couches for lounging, a dining table that's also perfect for spreading out the newspaper, a coffee table with a ready chess board, and plenty of good books to read.

[*RIGHT*] Skylights, white woodwork, and pale wood ceilings lighten up this cabin living space, where authentic western furniture and art feel right at home. You won't find a much sturdier upholstery fabric than a horse blanket; here it's combined with a collection of pillows covered in horsey prints and tongue-in-cheek zebra stripe; antler chandeliers and wrought iron table lamps provide warm overhead and accent lighting.

Bathing & Rejuvenating

It's hard to imagine that just one century ago, the average Old West bathroom was an unheated outdoor "privy," typically located fifty feet or more from the main house. The water for the weekly bath was heated on the wood stove, and several family members usually washed with the same tub of water. The modern bathroom has far surpassed its utilitarian roots, transforming our domestic rituals into times of both invigoration—with the rush of a bracing shower—and relaxation, during the quietude of an unhurried bath.

The master bathroom is often as luxurious as a spa, with amenities like rainhead or steam showers, large jetted soaking tubs, radiant floors, and even fireplaces. Some bathroom designers have updated the previous "standard" layout of a long, shared counter with double sinks; a two-person bath is sometimes arranged with separate vanities, individual mirror space, and additional storage.

Because safety is a prime concern when children are young, the family bathroom will likely include design choices like non-slip floor surfaces; shower doors of safety glass; a locking medicine cabinet; and an energy-efficient, thermostat-controlled hot water heater. Flooring and countertops of practical, water-resistant surfaces will withstand the inevitable splashes from the bathtub, and multigenerational families may need to build in safety measures like handrails for the needs of older family members.

Generally the smallest room in the house, the powder room, is one area where creative design can reign over daily practicalities. Unusual hardware and stylish fixtures can take center stage in the guest bathroom, and its windowless status allows for more intense color treatments and dramatic accessories.

Despite the wealth of amenities available in this century's bathroom, good water management is always a consideration in the western home. Many family bathrooms are fitted with low-flow showerheads, faucet aerators, and water-saving toilets that conserve precious resources while still providing the luxury of high-pressure water features.

[OPPOSITE] A vintage toy horse is the charming inspiration for this children's vanity area, where the custom twig cabinetry is offset by metalwork accents and hand-carved drawer pulls. The black door hardware reflects the horse's iron wheels as well as the custom western metalwork sconce, and walls the color of milk and honey contrast with the warm knotty pine trim. Textural interest comes from the soft, velvet upholstered slipper chair and woven sisal flooring—which is comfortable underfoot, but very durable.

[ABOVE] This open log home bathroom area provides plenty of contrast between light and dark elements. Because the walls are deep brown aged timber, the upper walls and ceiling were covered in a light pine paneling. White fixtures—including a traditional porcelain pedestal sink—brighten the space, and the simple white curtains allow for privacy while still letting in the sunlight. The outside of the claw foot bathtub is painted sage green; brass hardware includes a hand-held shower that is especially practical for washing children's hair. The rustic towel racks and shelves are handcrafted from twigs, and willow baskets hold extra towels. The floors are softened with Indian throw rugs.

[ABOVE] A cozy corner fireplace warms up this romantic bathroom, with a built-in jetted bathtub that just begs for a long, relaxing soak. A long ledge along the tub provides plenty of space for a row of flickering votive candles.

[ABOVE] An extra deep soaking tub creates a serene space to take in the breathtaking views surrounding this bathroom sanctuary. The textured walls are covered in a hand-troweled plaster veneer, and a stained concrete floor is beautiful, but also impervious to water. Horizontal upper windows allow sunlight to flood into the room while maintaining privacy.

[RIGHT] Traditional and modern elements combine in this urban bathroom, where an old-fashioned claw foot bathtub is fitted with a brass gooseneck faucet and a handy tub rack for holding shampoo and bath toys. A French armchair is a comfortable place for a parent to relax while a child is bathing, and the nearby window can easily be opened to let in breezes. A modern, framed print accents the olive green upper walls, while the lower walls are covered in a durable, white enamel-painted wainscoting.

[LEFT] An oversize mirror helps visually enlarge the room, and reflects the light from the windows on the opposite wall.

[BELOW] Simply elegant, a matching pair of raised white porcelain basins is mounted on a natural wood countertop, with the hardware mounted directly to the wall. Instead of sconces, vanity lighting is provided by eye-level lamps. Beyond the vanity, steps lead to a private, contemporary bathtub retreat.

[OPPOSITE] An alternative arrangement to a traditional countertop with dual sinks, a pair of pedestal sinks with separate mirrors and storage space creates a polished, symmetrical look. Tile floors and wainscoting painted in semi-gloss enamel can be easily cleaned.

[RIGHT] The faucet is mounted directly into the mirror in this organic space, creating a sense of water flowing from a secret source. A basin sink rests on a copper-covered countertop, and the natural stacked rock wall creates a divider between the vanity area and the master bedroom. No more folding bath towels into perfect thirds; instead, they dry quickly on wall-mounted hooks.

[LEFT] Calm and peaceful, this sunken tub has its own fireplace and a collection of flickering candles arranged on the surrounding black slate top. Instead of a tile or glass wall that has to constantly be cleaned, the adjacent rock wall is a maintenance-free surface—excellent for time-strapped parents—that is also a perfect backdrop for climbing plants.

[RIGHT] Countertops stay blissfully free from clutter in this rustic bathroom, where abundant two-toned cabinetry provides ample storage for toiletries and linens. Bronze hardware and brushed stainless bath and sink fixtures mix easily in this bathroom, disproving the outdated notion that everything has to match. Branches decorate the two barnwood-trimmed mirrors above the sinks, and a fold-out magnifying mirror makes it easy to put on makeup.

[LEFT] Instead of arranging the fixtures along the walls of this pristine, all-white bathroom, the clawfoot tub was placed at an angle—which in turn created a protected display space near the window for an antique urn. White tile in several patterns covers the floor and lower walls, while the upper walls and trim are painted a cool white. Color accents are provided by a fluffy bath rug and fun polka dot and fringe-trimmed towels.

[RIGHT] Soft beige and creamy white create a neutral color scheme in a bathroom that's bathed in natural sunlight. A glass-enclosed shower is tucked into a corner, leaving room for a built-in bathtub. The floor tile is laid on the diagonal, with tan accent dots that coordinate with the khaki tile trim on the backsplash and tub.

[*RIGHT*] Alice in Wonderland would be right at home in this whimsical bathroom, with its bold coral and white checkerboard tile walls and stylish built-in vanity. The homeowners were able to squeeze both a glass-enclosed corner shower and a bathtub in the room, and the curved cabinetry and a billowing balloon curtain create softness among the hard surfaces. A pair of stepstools makes it easier for little ones to reach the sink, and a soft floral rug feels good underfoot.

[RIGHT] The antiqued wood inlays in this vanity area's distinctive custom cabinetry are accented by a timeworn old chair and a pair of primitive masks. The plantation blinds on the dividing wall windows can be opened to let in additional light.

[ABOVE] The vertical ironwork mirror fits perfectly in this tall space, while horizontal contrast is provided by the square basin sink and its dry-stacked rock base.

[RIGHT, BOTTOM] A carved marble basin is the striking focal point of this vanity, with a small glass shelf mounted over the faucet to hold found objects and small paintings. The worn, vintage mirror is complemented by a hand-carved wooden cup and other antique pieces.

[LEFT] Forget postcards and t-shirts; this family found a better souvenir to remind them of jolly old London, installing one of the city's trademark red telephone booths in the powder room. Fitted with shelves and wired with a light, it serves as a one-of-a-kind linen closet. Because powder rooms are often located in interior, window-less spaces, bold color, such as this room's bright green, can often be used to great advantage; good lighting and ventilation are also key considerations.

[*ABOVE*] The carved sandstone sink and plaster walls create a neutral backdrop for the dramatic tooled metal-work mirror, and a light was cleverly hidden behind the arched cutout on top. To avoid hanging hardware on the walls that would distract from the mirror, the homeowners found a small standing rack for guest towels.

[*LEFT*] You won't find a vanity like this on every street corner, with its exotic burled wood trim and twig detailing. Commissioning high-end custom cabinetry might be too pricey for a larger room, but in a small space like a powder room it creates a huge impact. The faux leather finish on the walls is created with torn pieces of kraft paper.

BRIGHT IDEA

If your powder room gets a lot of traffic, install a knocker on the door so a guest can give a polite tap to make sure the room isn't already occupied before entering. This bathroom has arched plastered walls infused with a muted peach pigment that contrasts nicely with the antique look of the carved stone sink. Old-fashioned brass hardware is mounted directly into the wall, and a rack of patterned guest towels provides accent color.

Slumbering & Awakening

Whether it's a cozy attic room or a large master suite, a comfortable, stylish place to sleep is crucial for every member of the family. The adult bedroom is often the only real sanctuary away from the demands and clutter of the home, and it deserves to be serene, calm, and intimate. The defining design element of the western master bedroom is often its very setting, as architects tend to position this room to best take advantage of surrounding views and light.

The other natural focal point of the room is the usually its largest piece of furniture—the bed. And since we spend a third of our lives sleeping, choosing a good mattress is a critical decision. Parents are usually sleep-deprived during the early years of child raising (and again during the teenage years!), so anything that aids in inducing slumber will help make the room more relaxing and soothing: luxurious linens, perfect pillows, soft, sound-absorbing furnishings and floor coverings; and room-darkening window coverings to block the early morning light. Special photographs, books, and art can all add to the personal intimacy of the room.

Children's bedrooms provide an opportunity for youngsters to begin expressing their unique personalities and interests. Whenever possible, let children have input on their bedroom color, theme, and design elements and invest in good quality, versatile furniture pieces and practical flooring that can serve different roles as the child grows up. A child's play area can eventually transition to a sleepover or "hang out" space, and the right desk can grow up with the child, offering space for creative pursuits now and homework in future years.

Guestrooms provide a haven for overnight visitors, and their limited use can allow for extra creativity in color and design schemes. Bunkrooms can be a practical arrangement for those who host an abundance of visitors, and some families even create a separate guest house for additional privacy. Guest rooms that are as restful and inviting as the other bedrooms in the home will convey a sense of warmth and welcome.

[OPPOSITE] Colorful yet soothing, a bedroom painted soft mint green features a sturdy iron bed topped with an old-fashioned rainbow-hued patchwork quilt. Framing a beautiful outside view, a simple window is flanked by original paintings of landscapes.

[RIGHT] A daybed doubles as a seating area in this multi-purpose guest room that is restful with its azure walls combined with blue and white linens. A stepstool is handy for both youngsters and older people who might need a boost to climb into the tall bed.

[*OPPOSITE*] A study in contrast, this unusual hand-painted antique bed is tucked under a peaked window beneath the eaves, where white linens are offset by the dark wood of the antiques. Notice the various textures in the sunny space, too: the nubby white chenille covering the easy chair, the diamond-patterned rug underfoot, and the shiny striped satin on the bedside table.

[*RIGHT*] This master bedroom has a comfortable seating area for reading the morning paper and relaxing, and the parents can watch the children play in the enclosed courtyard outside. The whitewashed beams and iron cross look right at home paired with the plantation style four-poster bed.

[*BELOW*] The sheer curtains can be pulled around this iron framed bed to create a sense of privacy.

[*ABOVE*] Antique candelabras, jewelry, pillboxes, and a faded, vintage mirror create a striking arrangement on a mother's old-fashioned dressing table.

[OPPOSITE] The distinctive, ornately carved blue-green bed in this room is what interior designers sometimes call a "showstopper," a strong focal point that drives the design scheme in this largely neutral bedroom space. A carefully planned palette of colors and patterns includes greens, reds, browns, and blues that blend together seamlessly; the patterned easy chair and ottoman is a comfortable spot for reading a bedtime story.

[ABOVE] The windows were positioned up high to let in the light but maintain privacy in this bedroom that blends both traditional and eclectic elements. The walls are painted an unexpected spring green, and a pair of mounted antlers and two cozy reading lamps accent the purposely mismatched nightstands. [ABOVE RIGHT] A small antique desk is tucked in this bedroom, perfect for answering e-mails or catching up on correspondence. [RIGHT] Could you paint your wood trim hot pink? It takes nerve, but the bright color contrasts beautifully with the turquoise patterned bed linens and translucent glass lamps in this southwestern bedroom.

[*OPPOSITE*] A quick lesson in color theory: look at the impact the red accents make in this log-ceiling room, with its red Indian rugs, bed throw pillows, and the contrasting band of color across the bottom of the drapes.

[*ABOVE*] Morning light filters into a spacious master bedroom, where a large red Oriental rug provides space definition and brings color into the neutral-toned space. An oversize chaise lounge is positioned so that the parents can watch what's going on outside while reading or relaxing, and a tray-topped table at the end of the bed holds books and magazines that might otherwise create clutter.

[*OPPOSITE*] This bedroom is fit for a modern-day princess, and rather than trying to hide the space's urban loft elements the homeowners incorporated them into the design scheme. Walls were painted a vivid violet, and a hand-painted mural of a castle looks just right against the old weathered brick. Puffy clouds hang from the old beams, which are accented by the rustic wood frame of the curvy carved sleigh bed.

[*ABOVE*] A wicker day bed topped with an eyelet coverlet and a collection of patterned throw pillows are accented with walls and accessories of soft yellow in this charming bedroom. A bedside basket stores the ever-growing collection of stuffed animals and teddy bears.

[*LEFT*] Hey Diddle Diddle, have you ever seen a tufted chair—shaped like the moon? The dish runs off with the spoon on the hand-painted mural set against walls of pale green in this whimsical nursery scene; the white storage hutch is a basic piece that can easily transition as the child grows up.

[ABOVE] Why pay extra for a faux distressed finish, when you can acquire the real thing through daily living? These traditional bunk beds are painted antique red, and whether the distressing is real or faux is anyone's guess; a basket holds extra pillows for overnight visitors.

[RIGHT] Even grownups appreciate spending the night in these heavy log bunk beds. Indirect lighting hidden in the rafters gives the room a warm glow, and extra blankets for chilly nights are stashed in the trunk at the end of the bed.

BRIGHT IDEA

[ABOVE] A roomful of built-in bunk beds is the perfect way to accommodate a houseful of guests—especially children, who seem to love the "hideaway" feeling of separate bunks. Wainscoting and individual sconces create a cozy atmosphere inside each bunk space; guests can tuck their belongings in the rope-handled drawers beneath. *[TOP LEFT]* In this rustic log bunk room, safety is paramount with railings incorporated in the design of each bunk.

[LEFT] In the knotty pine paneled guest room, an open floorplan allows the room to serve other purposes, and abundant storage is incorporated under the normally-wasted space under the beds.

93

[OPPOSITE] A classic color scheme of red, tan, and blue looks fresh combined with the lighthearted house painting and an unusual hand-painted red dresser. The trick to successfully mixing stripes and floral fabrics like these is to stay within the same color range when combining the patterns.

[ABOVE] For a truly private reading (and daydreaming) nook, the curtains can be drawn around the cushioned window seat; storage space is built in underneath. With a pair of handsome matching bamboo beds like these, it's easy to have a friend over to spend the night.

[RIGHT] Here's an example of how one strong element can create a theme for a whole room (and no, it's not the family's dog); in this case, the painted insets on the beds inspired moose mania in the accompanying "Moose Crossing" signs, lamp base, and stuffed moose collection.

[ABOVE] Bold checked fabric is used on the iron bedframe curtains, picking up the blue and white of the bed's piecework quilt in this cozy cabin bedroom, where primitive art and a Craftsman-style lamp look right at home.

[LEFT] Silk curtains are draped invitingly around this exotic carved bed, where the colors, patterns, and textures are decidedly bold but within the same analogous color scheme: pink and white striped and floral patterned bed linens; a collection of silk-covered pillows (including one trimmed in feathers); eye-popping red walls; and a bright red and orange rug.

[OPPOSITE] Relaxing comes naturally in this restful, country-style guest room with an ironwork inset sleigh bed covered in layers of quilts and soft pillows. The lampshades, drapes, and coverlet are complementary red and white striped and checked fabrics that work together to create a unified look. A wreath of natural twigs hangs over the bed, accenting the unstained window trim and wooden curtain rods.

Enjoying the Outdoors

The phrase "The Great Outdoors" was surely coined in the West, where outdoor living is such an integral part of our lifestyle. Because our western architecture often draws its influence from the surrounding countryside, homes in this region are commonly designed with living spaces that blur the boundaries between inside and outside.

Whether it's a deck, patio, dock, courtyard, or porch, a comfortable outdoor living area is an extension of the home that lets families get out in the fresh air to play, relax, or simply drink in the open skies.

Westerners hold tight to the belief that food always tastes better when it's eaten outside, so most family homes include an area for dining al fresco. (From a practical standpoint, outside meals also mean less worry about spills and messes.) The barbeque grill—once relegated to summer cookouts—is now a staple in most households and increasingly used year-round. Comfortable, weatherproof seating and a covered roof or large umbrella for shade allow for easy, spontaneous outdoor dining and entertaining.

Even with an active family, it's possible to have an attractive landscape that's also practical and durable. Busy families may prefer sturdy, low maintenance plants and shrubs when time is at a premium. An area of hardy grass with room to play, and a dedicated dog run or animal play area will keep the primary lawn looking better. Children often enjoy digging in the dirt, and a vegetable garden can provide not only food for the family, but also valuable lessons about where our food comes from and how plants grow.

In warmer climates, a swimming pool is a sparkling landscape element that provides both family recreation and relief from the heat. In high altitude regions—where even summer evenings can be chill—an outdoor fireplace can extend the season of open-air living, while a hot tub is an amenity that seems to be appreciated by people in all seasons and climates.

[OPPOSITE] A pair of rocking chairs is the perfect spot to take in the scenery and listen to the sound of the wind in the trees. The twig side table has a built-in basket in the base, perfect for storing magazines and children's books to read at a moment's notice.

[*ABOVE*] A trio of deck chairs stands ready for a sunny afternoon siesta on this rock patio; the family dog has already claimed a napping spot in the cool shade.

[*LEFT*] If a picture is worth a thousand words, this scene sums up why people move from the city to the high country: a pair of Adirondack chairs on a rock patio creates a serene setting overlooking breathtaking views of the lake, forest, and mountains.

[*RIGHT*] A collection of rocking chairs beckons on this sunny deck, a fine spot to wrap up in a blanket and enjoy the day's first cup of coffee. Even on the hottest summer days, the cool breezes blow up from the mountain lake below. A vintage Cruz Blanca beer cooler is recycled as a plant stand.

[*BELOW*] When he's not posing for the camera, the home-owners' pet Weimaraner likes to sneak into the hot tub for a swim.

[*OPPOSITE*] This family never needs to load up the car with picnic gear or haul a heavy basket to a secluded spot; instead, they enjoy an easy change of scene for a fun meal at the ultimate picnic table setting just outside the door, overlooking glorious vistas in every direction.

[*ABOVE*] This patio area is ideal for outdoor entertaining, and the generously-sized stainless steel barbeque grill was built into the stone surround; protected from the elements, it can be used year-round.

[*LEFT*] Baby, it's cool outside—under the shade of this rustic deck; an assortment of weathered chairs and a well-worn coffee table create an inviting arrangement that's comfortable no matter what the thermometer reads.

[*ABOVE*] With a view of a meadow of wildflowers, this large table is perfect for family meals and entertaining. While it's always best to keep outdoor furniture in a protected space, these wicker and log chairs are tough enough to withstand the occasional afternoon thunderstorm.

[*LEFT*] Overlooking the always-changing panorama of the mountain sky, a sturdy table and chairs are put into service for breakfast, cocktails, and intimate dinners in this stunning lakeside setting.

BRIGHT IDEA

[*OPPOSITE*] City dwellers can borrow high country elements to make outdoor living areas cool and serene; even if you don't live by a babbling brook you can recreate the gentle sounds with a wall-mounted recirculating fountain like this one. An umbrella over the outdoor table provides shade when the midday sun is at its brightest. Limited gardening space? Container gardens are a great way to add color to a patio area, and they can be moved around to catch the sunlight or to a sheltered spot during an afternoon hail storm.

[LEFT] Amidst the tall grass on a late summer's day, a backyard picnic table is set with a simple lunch and a vase of cattails picked nearby.

[OPPOSITE] The bright blue of the home's exterior is echoed in the cool square stones of the patio, a lovely setting for a summer breakfast on the round glass table surrounded by French café-style chairs.

[ABOVE] It's a miniature jungle for youngsters who explore the narrow path surrounding this southwestern backyard. Native wildflowers and hardy perennials create a bright profusion of color in the free-form garden, barely contained within the courtyard's adobe walls.

[OPPOSITE] A western flower garden is the last place you'd expect to encounter a friendly elephant, but it's the surprise factor of this outdoor sculpture that makes the discovery so delightful in the dappled shade.

BRIGHT IDEA   [BELOW] A sturdy chair or bench can often make the transition to the outdoors; just sand the surface with medium sandpaper, give it a coat of primer, and paint it with several coats of exterior grade enamel. Move the piece under the shade of your favorite tree and let the garden grow around it, adding a few stepping stones to make it easier to get to. Bring the piece inside or cover it during harsh weather months to extend its life.

[*ABOVE*] A stepped stone path leads from the patio to the banks of a gentle brook, where a fetching bronze sculpture of four children fishing from a log is a charming surprise.

[*LEFT*] Stone steps lead down to a simple landing area, where a canoe is ready to push off into the sparkling azure waters of a mountain lake.

[*BELOW*] Whether you're canoeing, swimming, fishing, or merely sitting on the dock and dangling your feet in the water, a private pond offers plenty of ways to cool off at this secluded mountain home.

[RIGHT] No one will argue about taking a nap when it's in this lazy, gardenside hammock under the trees. Simple additions to the yard, such as this hammock, make the space more likely to be used by all.

BRIGHT IDEA

[BELOW] Careful thought went into the planning of this outdoor pool, which was sited below an upper deck so parents can keep an eye on the area. The brickwork surrounding the pool is a low-maintenance, non-slippery surface, and the fences were planted with vines to enclose the area and create privacy. The hot tub is located adjacent to the pool, and its surrounding landscaping shields the area from view.

[ABOVE] This wood-burning firepit is a simple way to enjoy the warmth and ambiance of a crackling fire on the patio. As an alternative to a permanent pit, a free-standing metal unit or a three-legged clay *chiminea* can also provide a smaller, more portable means of enjoying a fire outside.

[BELOW] A bonfire blazes in this simple outdoor rock fire circle—pass the marshmallows!

[RIGHT] The family's Golden Retriever has already claimed the best spot in front of the outdoor stone hearth, a luxurious amenity that enables everyone to spend more time on the patio despite cool evenings or changing weather. Even on summer nights, a fire can take the chill off the air and provide warmth and light; a few blankets on the chairs are also a thoughtful touch.

Retreating

When each member of the family has a separate place to get away from the demands of life and explore individual pursuits, there is balance in the home. The space can be as simple as a comfortable chair in a quiet corner to curl up and read a book or as elaborate as an artist's studio in an outbuilding. A sanctuary to pursue hobbies, relax, work, read, play, and unwind during leisure time will lead to less stress, more peace—and a happier household.

Where space is at a premium, little-used spaces in the home can sometimes double as retreat areas; a guest room can do double duty as a sewing area, for instance. Even utilitarian spaces like garages and sheds can be transformed into getaways with the right furnishings and accessories.

Dad's traditional book-lined den may be as rare as *Leave it to Beaver* reruns, but its replacement—the home office—is now commonplace in most western homes. The advances in technology mean that we can often work from virtually any location, a development that families with small children often use to their advantage. Whether one works from home or just needs a quiet place to pay bills and manage household affairs, a dedicated space helps keep paperwork—and expensive equipment such as computers and printers—separate and safe from the little hands and sticky fingers of curious explorers.

Just as adults need retreat spaces, a dedicated play area for children is an arrangement that benefits everyone in the family. Noise can be contained within a playroom, storage can be designed to hold the myriad small pieces from toys and games, and surfaces can be installed to facilitate worry-free creative pursuits. Playrooms designed with flexible floor plans and versatile furniture can adapt to changing interests and varying activities, and help create an atmosphere where imagination has plenty of room to grow.

[TOP RIGHT] Who says the silver tea set has to stay packed away for special occasions? Fresh flowers picked from the garden look just right casually arranged in a shiny sterling teapot.

[OPPOSITE] This "room with a view," is a quiet getaway where adults can slip away to drink a cup of coffee or read the morning paper. The French doors are fitted with glass, allowing parents (or grandparents) to block out noise but still see into the next room.

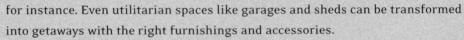

[LEFT] A stack of board games stands at the ready, perfect for a lazy afternoon.

[BELOW, LEFT] Sunny and bright, this corner retreat features an overstuffed easy chair and a comfortable chaise lounge that's large enough to stretch out on and take a catnap.

[BELOW, RIGHT] Sometimes a little-used corner of a room can be set up as a retreat area. Here, a cushion-covered wicker chair is arranged to face a restful view out the window; a small side table holds a vintage bar set.

[LEFT] Cool and breezy, this screened-in porch lets the family enjoy the outdoors while keeping the bugs and weather at bay; the fireplace warms the space on chilly evenings.

[RIGHT] A home office space with style blends an antique writing desk and old-fashioned Tiffany-style lamp with a modern chair and a framed painting of a tranquil scene.

[ABOVE] The bright blue back wall and a bold wall covering complement this contemporary room's clean, spare design—ideal for a tidy home office dweller. A drawerless Parsons-style desk eliminates clutter, and a file cabinet behind the desk holds necessary papers.

[RIGHT] A paper-saver's dream come true, this office is outfitted with row after row of convenient built-in drawer space. With all the storage problems solved, all that's left to face—besides the day's work—is the beautiful view out the eye-level windows.

[ABOVE, LEFT] Old 45 records are affixed to the stairway wall, giving a hint of the basement room's design theme. A working jukebox is a popular draw with kids of all ages in this 50s-inspired "rumpus room," where the walls are decorated with framed LP records.

[ABOVE, RIGHT] A neon-topped bar features stools covered in eye-popping colors, a traffic light mounted on the wall, jars of penny candy, an old-fashioned radio, and a quirky collection of kitsch.

[LEFT] All that's missing is the soda jerk at this fountain-inspired counter, surrounded by red stools, a working jukebox, restaurant-style fixtures, and 50s memorabilia. The black and white tile floors are authentic—and easy to keep clean.

[OPPOSITE] This play area includes an inspired collection of retro furnishings: a Jetsons-style round swivel table; a pair of bright yellow chairs—one with an unusual attached side table; an old parking meter; a gum machine; a neon clock—and heavy duty, commercial-style carpeting.

[ABOVE] With plenty of room to maneuver even the trickiest shots, this pool table is surrounded by abundant windows to flood the space with natural light; a saloon-style three-light fixture illuminates the table's playing surface.

[RIGHT] A palette of neutral colors and fine materials create an oasis of calm in this contemporary, multipurpose room. Family members can play pool, watch television and movies, build a fire in the fireplace, spread out projects on the work table – or simply sit and take in the beautiful views from the expansive windows.

[ABOVE] It's outfitted like the finest private club, but believe it or not, this ultimate men's retreat was originally a garage. Now the space has an entire wall of gilt-framed televisions, a poker table surrounded by leather club chairs, and a billiards table. Luxurious touches include silk-draped windows, slate floors, and a pair of alabaster chandeliers.

[OPPOSITE]   Quiet, simple and serene, this private room—complete with its own comfortable pew—is a sanctuary for meditation and prayer.

[RIGHT]   Just a few steps above the great room, this open craft/sewing room lets Mom work on projects without being isolated from the family activities nearby. She also has the best view in the house out her window by the sewing machine.

[BELOW, LEFT]   A charming arched doorway leads to a quiet getaway, perfect for practicing music, reading, or just watching the wildlife from the comfortable window seat.

[BELOW, RIGHT]   Children need time to relax and recharge their batteries, too. A piece of floor and a patch of sunlight is perfect for a reading break.

[*ABOVE*] An artist's studio offers abundant storage for supplies, plus large tables to spread out work. Plenty of comfortable seating allows the space to double as an additional living area.

[*OPPOSITE*] For a dedicated gardener, an area to pot plants and arrange cut flowers is a practical luxury that helps keep messy tasks out of living areas. A coat rack and bench by the door serve as an informal changing station, and washable rugs accommodate muddy feet. A peg rack holds the owner's impressive collection of gardening hats.

[*LEFT*] It looks old, but this wagon was hand-built by artisan Lynn Sedar using drawings and photos of a century-old gypsy van. Not an inch is wasted inside the elegant wagon, where a comfortable bed—perfect for an afternoon nap or accommodating an overnight guest— shares space with a writing desk, working sconce lights, and a small hot plate to brew a pot of tea.

[*BELOW*] A sheepwagon is parked in a remote part of this family's property, and with no signs of civilization around the scene looks much like it did a century ago. The wagon's weathered exterior hides a secret, though; inside, it's outfitted with oppulence.

BRIGHT IDEA

[ABOVE] If your property includes a lake or stream for fishing, why not do what this family did and build a fishing cabin right on the property? Just down the hill from the main residence, this charming stone outbuilding is a home-away-from-home for the family fishermen, and it can also be pressed into duty as a guest house if needed.

[LEFT] Whenever the urge to go fishing strikes, a collection of wicker creels is ready to go.

acknowledgements

*"With an eye made quiet by the power of harmony, and the deep power of joy,
we see into the life of things."*

—WILLIAM WORDSWORTH

To photographers Gordon Gregory, Audrey Hall, Linda Hanselman, Heidi Long, Daniel Nadelbach, Dave Rosenberg, and Pam Singleton: your beautiful images brought this project to life, and you were each a delight to work with. Thank you.

To the homeowners who opened their doors and allowed their homes to be photographed, thank you for your generosity and western hospitality.

To managing editor Claudine Randazzo: Your brilliant ideas, keen insights, and thoughtful suggestions made this project a collaboration of the highest order, and I am grateful and fortunate for the opportunity to work with you.

To Dave Jenney and Larry Lindahl: Your beautiful layouts brought me to tears in Flagstaff, and your creativity and passion for the book show on every page. Thank you.

Thanks to Irene Rawlings, Loneta Showell, and Christine DeOrio at *Mountain Living* magazine for blazing the trail and setting the standard for excellence. Every writer needs a trusted reader and sounding board, and I am eternally grateful to talented writers Darla Worden, Anne McGregor Parsons, and Gail Riley for your expertise and support, and especially for your friendship.

resources

Fisher Custom Homes
7500 E. Pinnacle Peak Rd.,
Building G-120
Scottsdale, AZ 85255
(480) 585-7350
www.fishercustomhomes.com

Len Ford
Ford Construction
538 Willow Glen
Kalispell, MT 59901
(406) 755-5224

Dennis Kelleher
Kelleher's General Contracting
P.O. Box 1676
Bigfork, MT 59911
(406) 756-5860
www.kellehercontracting.com

Kinnerbuilt Homes
501 E. 1st Ave.
Denver, CO 80203
(720) 620-0222

Tom LaChance
LaChance Builders
304 Wisconsin Ave.
Whitefish, MT 59937
(406) 862-5597
www.lachancebuilders.com

Casey Malmquist
Malmquist Construction
335 Spokane Ave.
Whitefish, MT 59937
(406) 862-7846
www.malmquist.com

Doug McDowell
McDowell Construction
Santa Fe, NM
(505) 982-5238

Bruce Olson Construction
7320 River Rd.
Olympic Valley, CA 96146
(530) 581-1087

Mars Combes
Spanish Peaks Construction Co.
22580 County Rd 437
Aguilar, CO 81020-9720
(719) 941-4272

Swanson Construction, Inc
P.O. Box 6538
Bozeman, MT 59771
(406) 587-8200
www.SwansonConstruction.net

Yellowstone Traditions
P.O. Box 1933
Bozeman, MT 59771
(406) 587-0968
www.YellowstoneTraditions.com

[INTERIOR DESIGNERS]

Linda Applewhite & Associates
510 Turney St.
Sausalito, CA 94965
(415) 331-2040
www.lindaapplewhite.com

Diana Beattie Interiors
1136 Fifth Ave.
New York, NY 10128
(212) 722-6226

Paula Bennett Design Studio
3184 So. Vine Ct.
Englewood, CO 80113
(303) 733-0344

Sher Colquitt Designs
5 La Otra Vanda
Santa Fe, NM 87540
(505) 992-0090

Oren Bishop, ASID
DMJM Design
2777 E. Camelback Rd., Suite 200
Phoenix, AZ 85016
(602) 337-2571
Oren.Bishop@dmjmhn.aecom.com

Design Associates
962 Stoneridge, Suite 1
Bozeman, MT 59718
(406) 582-8979
www.dainteriors.com

Roger Bailey
Design Co PnL
2911 Walnut St
Denver, CO 80205
(303) 291-1163
DesignCoPnL@aol.com

Design Works
19 W. Babcock
Bozeman, MT 59715
(406) 582-0222
www.designworksmt.com

Mary Butzke Bishop, ASID
ethos
302 No. 1st Ave., Suite 120
Phoenix, AZ 85003
(602) 256-6949
mbishop@ethosphx.com

Inter Plan Design Group
7373 N. Scottsdale Rd., Suite A-178
Scottsdale, AZ 85253
(480) 443-3400

Julie Fletcher
Interiors by Julie Fletcher, Inc.
963 South Jamaica St.
Aurora, CO 80012
(303) 364-8877

Patricia Gorman Associates
4319 Main St.
Philadelphia, PA 19127
(215) 482-1820
www.patriciagorman.com

Gilda Meyer-Niehof
Jadu Design
P.O. Box 24354
Santa Fe, NM 87502
(505) 982-7004
www.coyoacan.com

Kristi Dinner
KD Design Consultants
787 Elizabeth St.
Denver, CO 80206
(303) 355-1840
www.kddesignconsultants.com

La Puerta Design Originals
4523 State Rd., Highway 14
Santa Fe, NM 87508
(505) 984-8164
www.lapuertaoriginals.com

Lane Elizabeth Oliver Interior
Design, Inc.
881 So. York St.
Denver, CO 80209-4646
(303) 722-4288

Susan K. Okamoto, Inc
2300 7th Ave.
Seattle, WA 98121
(206) 324-8161

Roger Parrish
Edward Parent & Associates, Inc.
645 Walnut St.
Boulder, CO 80302
(303) 442-1905

Laurel Quint
Q Design
1337 Bellaire St.
Denver, CO 80220
(303) 778-7072
www.qinteriordesign.com

Margie McCullough
Red Pepper Kitchen + Bath
726C Pearl St.
Boulder, CO 80302
(303) 413-9400
www.redpepdesign.com

Linda Seeger
Linda Seeger Interior Design
4342 N. Civic Center Plaza
Scottsdale, AZ 85251
(480) 348-2776
www.seegerinteriordesign.com

Carole Sisson Design
117 E. Main St.
Bozeman, MT 59715
(406) 587-2600
www.SissonDesigns.com

S. Trowbridge & Co.
1012 Marquez Place
Suite 209A
Santa Fe, NM 87505
(505) 995-8214
strowbridgeco@earthlink.net

[OTHER RESOURCES]

Lazy Moose Ranch
2455 N. Fish Creek Rd.
P.O. Box 1430
Wilson, WY 83014
(307) 739-2276
www.lazymooseranchllc.com

Moonlight Basin
P.O. Box 160040
Big Sky, MT 59716
(406) 993-6000
www.moonlightbasin.com

Lynn Sedar
Ranch Willow Wagon Co.
501 U.S. Highway 14
Sheridan, WY 82801
(307) 674-1510
www.ranchwillowwagons.com

Russell & Rusty Viers
Viers Furniture Company
65 Billman Lane
Livingston, MT 59047
(406) 222-7564
www.montanawesternfurn.com

Yellowstone Club
P.O. Box 161097
Big Sky, MT 59716
(406) 995-4900
 www.yellowstoneclub.com

[PHOTOGRAPHERS]

Gordon Gregory Photography
2807 Allison Ct.
Bozeman, MT 59718
(406) 556-9854
www.GordonGregoryPhoto.com

Audrey Hall Photography
1106 W. Park St., #121
Livingston, MT 59047
(406) 222-2450
www.audreyhall.com

Linda Hanselman
Hanselman Photography
388 Emerson St.
Denver, CO 80218
(303) 861-5520
llhanselman@yahoo.com

Douglas Kahn Photography
P.O. Box 1430
Westcliffe, CO 81252
(719) 783-9733
www.douglaskahnphoto-
grapher.com

Heidi A. Long
Longviews Studios
1116 Second Ave. W.
Kalispell, MT 59901
(406) 756-1489
www.longviews.com

Daniel Nadelbach, Photographer
Gilda Meyer-Niehof, Stylist
Daniel Nadelbach Photography,
LLC
P.O. Box 24354
Santa Fe, NM 87502
(505) 982-7004
www.nadelbachphoto.com
www.coyoacan.com

Dave Rosenberg
Dave Rosenberg Photography
2565 So. Gilpin St.
Denver, CO 80210
(303) 893-0893
www.daverosenberg.com

Pam Singleton
Image Photography
P.O. Box 783
Scottsdale, AZ 85252
(480) 946-3246
www.photoexcursions.com

This list includes a sampling of vendors, and the publisher is not liable for errors or omissions.

134

photo credits

Photography © 2006 by:

This list includes a sampling of vendors, and the publisher is not liable for errors or omissions.